BEAT HIM AT HIS OWN DIVORCE!

By

Ted Knight

Thornsbury Bailey & Brown, Inc.
P. O. Box 5169, Arlington, VA 22205

Beat Him At His Own Divorce!

Manufactured in the United States of America.

Published by:
Thornsbury Bailey & Brown, Inc.
Post Office 5169
Arlington, VA 22205
(Fax: 703-532-0704)

ISBN: 0-945253-13-3

Disclaimer:
It is not intended that this document provide any legal, financial or other professional advice. The suggestions contained herein are only offered for consideration by the reader based upon the author's experience in observing how they helped other women during their divorces. Not all suggestions are universally applicable to each divorce situation. The reader is advised to seek professional assistance concerning the specific issues of her divorce and understands that all divorces have their unique characteristics.

PLANNING A SEMINAR?

Yes, please have Ted Knight contact me about conducting a seminar for my group/organization on how to *Beat Him At His Own Divorce!*

Your Name: _____ Phone: _____

Your Organization's Name: _____

Address: _____

State: _____ Zip: _____ Fax: _____

Number Attending: _____ Desired Dates: _____

Please return this form to Ted Knight, c/o TBB, Inc., Post Office Box 5169, Arlington, VA 22205 well in advance of your planned event (Fax: 703-532-0704 or tnight@erols.com).

WHY NOT HELP OUT A FRIEND?

Ted, I have a friend and she could benefit from a copy of your book. Please send *Beat Him At His Own Divorce!* to:

Friend's Name: _____

Friend's Address: _____

I am including my check to TBB, Inc. for $14.95 + $3 s/h for a single copy.

I want to send _____copies. Enclosed is my check for $14.95 per copy and I'll let you pay for the shipping and handling! Please send them to the enclosed mailing list in my name.

BEAT HIM AT HIS OWN DIVORCE!

By Ted Knight

FOREWORD

Divorce is a fact of life in America. It has increased to the point that about half of the misty-eyed newly-wed couples who walked down the aisle in the '90s will make an encore appearance at the domestic courts ending their union a few short years later. Perhaps it should be no real surprise that this relaxed attitude about marriage has overflowed from the newly-wed set to the owners of marriage licenses issued three and four decades ago with much the same result. In fact, divorce among spouses married for several decades is the fastest growing category of divorce.

It is also a fact that the quality of life of men, at least financially, often does not suffer much as a result of divorce, while that of their ex-wives frequently worsens. Economically, men continue to earn more and the divorce is often simply relegated to a financial settlement or monthly "bill" that they are willing to pay for their new-found freedom. Women often just don't fight to receive the settlements they need to rebuild their lives. Their husbands' divorces paralyze them.

How does it all get started? More and more men are having some form of "mid-life crisis" resulting in their need for "their own space" and often the abandonment of their family of two, three or even four decades. Characteristically, they strike out and acquire a faster and sportier car, new clothes, an apartment or some other get-away and, of course, a younger "trophy wife" or "trophy girlfriend". Their families become a burden or the enemy or just "them". Family relations are turned upside down. The word "loyalty" seems to have been removed from the American version of English. Children of these divorces (young and adult alike), often don't know what to say to their parents or their own kids.

These uncertainties sometimes manifest themselves in extremely large doses of self-blame, guilt, out-of-wedlock pregnancies of the daughters (perhaps seeking to get even) and tragically, suicides among adult sons. Mutual friends shed their "mutuality" not knowing what to say or not say. Often the wife is regarded as the carrier of some social plague that her peers, especially other wives, are certain is contagious. Meanwhile her soon-to-be "Ex" enjoys the double standard distinction of "stud duck" complete with all the accouterments of the knowing, often envious smiles from the men and erotic question marks in the minds of the women.

However the divorce begins, it is often the man leaving the woman. This book was written for the women who are left -- the deserted wives. Such is their repayment after decades of raising children, volunteering in the school and community, scouts, little league, school plays, late nights caring for the ill, training pets, trying to retain their bridal day figures and beauty, supporting their hubbies' professional endeavors and generally being the mainstay of their family.

Beat Him At His Own Divorce! is a different book. It is a book about empowerment for deserted wives.

It is not one of those "how-to-get-a-divorce", or "everything-you-ever-wanted-to-know-about-divorce" books. It won't guide you through the divorce process in your state. Nor does it contain any legal or accounting advice. You should not consider it a substitute for professional assistance. No right or wrong judgments are offered; rather observations about likely reactions to actions are put forth in as dispassionate a manner as possible.

This is a guide to *thinking* and using *logic* to manage something you never wanted in the first place -- his divorce! It is intended to give you a quick point of reference after the rug has been pulled out from under you. It offers advice for your actions when you first hear, "I want a divorce", through the property negotiation, and after the judge's gavel falls making you single again.

It provides you with a series of observations and ideas about the divorce process that can help you cope with some of the difficult issues you will be facing. It is intended to be an empowering resource that will make you stronger and more certain of your actions when your world seems to have been turned on its ear.

Beat Him At His Own Divorce!, was carefully chosen as the title of this book.

When the "light of your life" walks out the door to live with someone else there is little you can do to reverse the situation. Besides, do you really want to? Do you want someone who doesn't want you? Can you *really* trust him again? If after he comes back, he is late one night -- can you be sure it was due to an out-of-town client's visit and if it was, how can you be sure the client wasn't fetching in her low-cut tight cocktail dress?

This is where the logic must begin. Once he leaves -- he has left! It is very seldom that the damage can be repaired to the point you can return to "normal". All that remains is to get the best settlement you can and get on with your life. Yet this is the very essence of the difference between a man's and a woman's perceptions of divorce. If he leaves, you can bet he's been planning it for some time. And he has the edge. He's probably set aside money, changed his will, stocked his new abode with new clothes and all the comforts of life -- perhaps even your replacement.

Beat Him At His Own Divorce!, is a guide to help you keep your sanity during a time of insanity. It is intended to make you the winner -- if there is such a thing -- but at least not a complete loser.

v

The practical suggestions contained between these covers have their origins in business management and logic, devoid (as much as possible) of emotionalism which is admittedly difficult because divorce is an emotion-charged event. Remember, marriage is about *love* and divorce is about *money*.

Now before you ask, "How can business management techniques possibly help *me* in a divorce?", consider that these techniques have been tested with other women who have gone through the same or similar situations as you now face. They were tested working directly with several women (and observing several others) who after many decades found themselves abandoned for "trophy wives" in very high profile divorce cases. They sought advice from the author, a management consultant, about what to do and how to do it.

The lessons learned from those experiences are presented throughout the book. When followed, the better settlements were achieved. When not followed, the predicted outcomes were realized.

At times the techniques are presented with some humor which you may not fully appreciate at this time. As the process hardens your disappointment, feelings of abandonment and betrayal perhaps may make you just a bit more cynical and you may see some humor in your situation. You may even get a giggle or two -- believe it or not, you will relearn the art of laughter.

It should also be noted that the author is a man. He has never been divorced and doesn't ever intend to be -- if only for the reason that he has seen through others' experiences the pain and hurt it creates. However, as a man, he has heard that side of divorce. In the many places where men congregate, he has learned that for the exiting husband, divorce is simply a matter of how much it will cost and how he will be perceived by anyone whose opinion he may value, such as, his mother, his children, his boss, guys at the club, and, of course, the fortunate future occupants of his bed.

Also, the reader should realize that *Beat Him At His Own Divorce!* is more than just a book. The author would like it to be considered an on-going service to women who find themselves in the predicament of *his divorce*. Therefore, having purchased and read this book, each reader is entitled to contact the author if there are any questions about the material contained herein.

For women who cannot afford to hire a Project Manager, as is recommended in the book, the author will be happy to provide occasional (non-legal or non-accounting) free strategic advice. The author is also available to work with your local organizations to provide a one or two-day seminar on how to *Beat Him At His Own Divorce!* Seminars will require preplanning and do involve some fees.

The author, Ted Knight, may be contacted through the publisher, TBB, Inc., at Post Office Box 5169, Arlington, VA 22205 (fax: 703-532-0704). You may also contact him via his e-mail: tnight@erols.com. Be sure to include at least your first name, mailing address and phone/fax number or e-mail address.

So put on a pot of coffee, sit down and get ready to

Beat Him At His Own Divorce!

TABLE OF CONTENTS

1. *"HOW DID I EVER GET INTO THIS MESS?"*

Have you ever heard someone say, "If only I hadn't..." done something that could have prevented a tragedy? For example, "If only I hadn't asked her to go to the store she wouldn't have had the car wreck!" Or, "If I hadn't made him late for the first flight he wouldn't have been on the one that went down!"

This may sound weird, but it is a psychological fact that people need to feel they are in control. So they make statements of guilt at times of tragedy and by doing so hope to generate some false sense of control. In other words, they are willing to trade guilt for a pseudo feeling of control over circumstances that are really beyond their control. Silly isn't it? But it's true. It's human nature.

The same is true with divorce. Think how many times you may have heard a female friend who was confronted with what now is facing you say, "If I hadn't been so frivolous with money, maybe he'd have stayed." Or, "If I had been a better wife", or "greater lover", or "waited on him like his mom did", or...

It can go on and on and on. The simple fact is that you are in this mess *because he put you in it!* Oh, he might have some excuse he's using for public relations purposes, but the real truth of the matter is he left you and he probably was planning to do so for some time.

So the first thing you have to get straight is that *you did not do anything, it's not your fault!*

Now you have to make the best of a bad situation. Forget about Mr. Wonderful coming back, things being the way they were, or living the American dream with him. That's not to say you won't be able to weather the storm and have a happy life, but for the next couple of years you will be coping with his divorce -- mind you, it's not "our" divorce or "your" divorce -- it's "his" divorce. He started it and now you have to finish it -- a winner!

Winning is probably not the first thing in a woman's mind when confronted with being one half of the "team" in the divorce game. Initially there are some immediate emotions, the sense of loss and abandonment, anger and shame, as well as the uncertainties -- what to say to friends and family, how to handle the kids (young or adult), how to pay the bills, where to get an attorney, how to live without sex, how to get the home repairs done, and so forth. No one likes rejection.

When Mr. Wonderful suddenly leaves, you can bet it is only "suddenly" for you. He's probably been planning it for some time. Few husbands just up and leave on the spur of a moment. It might appear that way, but most likely he has been setting aside some resources, finding alternative living arrangements, ordering a new phone, starting a new bank account and all those other things that are needed to handle the immediate transition.

So there you are. He's left you and the kids. You feel lost, off balance and like someone just kicked you in the stomach. You are angry and hurt at the same time. You don't know where to begin. You are having trouble thinking and keeping your mind focused. Sleep eludes you nightly. You probably just want to crawl in a hole and pull the opening in after you.

Go ahead and take a week or so to feel sorry for yourself. Get your crying out of the way. Go somewhere remote and shout all the evil things you can think about him as loud as you can. If you enjoy kicking something or throwing plates, do so. Whatever helps you relieve the initial shock, do it -- short of shooting him! When that's over, pull yourself together, stand up on your own hind feet and

Beat Him At His Own Divorce!

14

2. FIRST THINGS FIRST

Who Files?

After he leaves, the fact is you are still married, until the divorce is completed and that means someone has to initiate the divorce -- file for divorce. Perhaps it is a male macho thing, but traditionally the wife is "allowed" to file as she is the offended party. This is especially true when older marriages break up. Supposedly it helps her to save face. You need to consider if you want to file or make him file.

One woman refused to file saying she didn't want the divorce, it was his idea, and *he* could just sever the marriage. Psychologically it did wonders! From that time on, the man of her dreams, was fighting an image problem with his children, family of origin, friends and business associates. Her strategy clearly marked him as the party causing the injury. His children knew he had left their mother and that he was responsible for breaking up the family. He paid dearly for it later in terms of their affections, willingness to hear his side of the issues and lack of family invitations during the holidays and special events.

Consult your attorney about the possible repercussions, but if you don't want the divorce, then don't be an enabler by making it easy on him. Make *him* file!

What Do You "Want" from the Divorce?

The second thing you need to do is figure out, after settling the filing issue, is exactly what it is you want from the divorce. *"But I never wanted this divorce in the first place!"*

Maybe not, but you're stuck with it and you have to make the best of a bad situation -- what's the expression, making lemonade from lemons? What you specifically want will be discussed later in

Chapter 6, *Setting Your Goals*, however, this is a good time to introduce who might be able to help you determine that in a realistic fashion.

It would be very helpful if you could find someone who is completely on your side, but dispassionate on the subject of Mr. Wonderful and his actions. This can be difficult and sometimes impossible. You probably don't really want a good friend because they know you and probably him from before and may bring with their well-meaning advice many of the same biases and perspectives that you do. That kind of reinforcement will not be helpful.

You need someone who can see the reality of the situation; a person who can be objective on your behalf. You need to hear when you have a bad idea or when your former live-in might, in fact, have a worthwhile point in some of his actions or statements. What you need is a person who provides you with as much impartial advice and information as possible when you need it and can keep you on track. You need a *Project Manager*.

Find a Project Manager

What's a project manager? This is a person who can see the entire picture, has the overall perspective of what is taking place and what still needs to be done. The project manager need not be, most likely won't be, and probably shouldn't be expert in all the technical areas of divorce. But he should be able to see that nothing falls through the cracks and that you get the support and resources you need to stay the course.

Your Attorney as a Project Manager?

Most often women put their attorneys in this role. They pay the retainer, expenses and hourly rates and basically turn everything over to him or her. This can have mixed results.

Traditional divorce attorneys handle many divorces and other legal matters simultaneously. They have many clients and the most successful attorneys are often the most expensive. The attorney/ project manager is not the best route to take. Attorneys' time is divided with other clients, they are expensive, they usually view everything in terms of the law and what the judge and opposing counsel will or won't do. The reality is that their view of your "best interests" can be influenced by many factors.

Another few words about traditional divorce attorneys need to be stated. Attorneys take a bad rap. Have you ever seen the bumper sticker "Shakespeare was right -- kill all the lawyers"? That is actually a misquote. Shakespeare wrote that if anarchy was desired that it could be achieved by killing all the lawyers. Unfortunately not all lawyers today are as noble as Shakespeare credited. But beyond that, there is a less philosophical and more practical concern.

Many divorce attorneys take advantage of the contrivances of modern technology and in doing so they use preprogrammed documentation such as pleadings, divorce settlement arrangements, and other various forms and documents. Sometimes they also use documentation from previous divorces and "tailor" them to your needs. With all this automation there is often a severe lack of attention paid to the details of your situation.

One woman found that the documents her Mr. Wonderful was transmitting were totally unintelligible. They were poorly written and made little sense. Furthermore, neither her soon-to-be-Ex nor his attorney even proof read them! So she had her Project Manager review them and develop a list of questions first about their meaning and then about their content. The resulting 12 pages gave Mr. Wonderful and his attorney cause to pause and reconsider their situation. Mr. Wonderful pressed with the divorce, but got another (his second of what was eventually three) attorney and realized that the little meek woman he abandoned meant business!

17

A second woman actually began worrying that her Mr. Wonderful's lawyer was screwing things up and then realized that she caught herself once more trying to make her husband look good. She had to be sure the opposing lawyer understood what hers was doing. In both cases these women had to do Mr. Wonderful's work and be certain the attorneys were sufficiently competent to get the divorce their Mr. Wonderfuls had started.

Your Accountant as a Project Manager?

Some women believe that accountants make good project managers. In cases involving large property settlements, it is true that a *forensic accountant* is very valuable. It has been said that accountant's fees are often a better divorce expenditure than attorney's fees. But again, accountants are busy and have lots of other clients. Like attorneys it is hard for them to be personally involved.

Your Spiritual Leader as a Project Manager?

Some women turn to their spiritual leaders to serve as project managers. But spiritual leaders are not fighters and when push comes to shove, you'll need a fighter, a schemer, a champion in your corner. You will need someone who can get tough advising you how to deal with Mr. Wonderful, your attorney, your accountant and anyone else who won't represent your best interests during the divorce.

Perhaps the strongest warning about using spiritual leaders as project managers is their mission in life. They help people solve their problems, and they often do this through compromise. If your family is a religious one, the pastor, priest or rabbi is probably friendly with both you and Mr. Wonderful -- hardly the objectivity you will be needing!

Get the Right Project Manager!

It is no literary license that has been observed in the preceding paragraphs in referring to your prospective project manager as "he".

You will need someone who can understand how Mr. Wonderful thinks. This may sound stereotypical and sexist. But the fact of the matter is men and women are different and think differently -- which is in part how you got in this mess in the first place! You will need to fight fire with fire.

So how do you pick a project manager?

You will need a man. You will need a clear thinker. You will need someone who will not replace your emotional ties with your departing husband -- don't fall in love with your Project Manager! You should pay a fee for his services which can be expensive. However that expense is probably no worse than the additional costs of the lawyer to whom you might have assigned this role in the first place. And if the person you select is good, you should save on your legal and accounting fees if only from the conserved time of exploratory investigations or tasks you can do together to get the information needed to fuel your side of the divorce.

If you cannot find a suitable project manager, you will have to do it yourself (or accept the author's offer in the *Foreword*). But that means you will need to be very analytical and force your emotions into the back seat. You should make a list of everything you want a project manager to do and decide what tasks you are comfortable with and which ones you will need to assign to others.

What Does Mr. Wonderful Want?
The man who is divorcing you is probably not the man you married.

When you married you were "in love" and love is a very blinding condition. You probably discussed the future, kids, your families, the life you'd share and many other rosy subjects. If he was raised in a traditional home during the 1940's and '50s, he probably saw his mother fuss over his father. Dad was "king of the castle" and life was not too dissimilar from the *Ozzie and Harriet* and *Father Knows Best* world that the new invention, television, portrayed. His role as bread-winner and stoic were almost inbred. As time went by, he became more and more isolated from you with his work and outside interests. The children might have become a burden only "to be seen and not heard" or acceptable to him when they were "clean and not crying". It is common knowledge that marriage, work, raising children and life in general are forces that change people. Sound familiar?

Somewhere along the line he probably looked in the mirror and realized that time was catching up with him -- a mid-life crisis! His youth was waning. His friends might have divorced or become separated. Younger, trimmer, more curvaceous women began catching his eye. Perhaps he even had an affair or two along the way. Whatever the actual situation that confronts you, his exodus was probably building for some time.

So what does he want? He wants his "freedom". He wants his "space". He probably wants to regain his youth, but so do we all! He wants to settle his debt with you on a financial basis, not an emotional one, and he comes to view the entire divorce as a financial transaction that needs to be negotiated. He may care enough about the kids to want to remain in touch. He may even want to continue to look good in their eyes.

He may tell you or others that he wants to be "generous" to you. What's generous? It took two of you to say "I do" -- didn't it? There were two of you in the marriage -- right? Presumably it took two of you to create those lovely children -- or was there some form of immaculate conception involved? It now takes two of you to separate and end the marriage -- definitely! So it is only reasonable that you divide your worldly possessions by two. So "generous" is anything in excess of the one-half of your combined worldly worth, which you have probably more than earned by now.

Now there is an exception to this definition of "generous". If you have always been the breadwinner or came into the marriage with wealth, the last thing you want to do is pay him alimony or give him any of your riches. In this case, "generous" is letting him exit without him paying too many penalties and "reasonable" is keeping what was yours in the first place! Why should he profit from making you miserable?

One woman had this problem but it was quickly resolved by some home videos taken through his window, with his little "bon-bon" reenacting the more imaginative scenes found on the backroom shelves at the local video store! She didn't pay a cent and kept everything! Presumably he continued the amateur antics of the celluloid with his young vixen!

3. WHAT MADE MR. WONDERFUL SO WONDERFUL?

Now before you go any further, it is advisable for you to take a few moments and remember what it was that made Mr. Wonderful wonderful in the first place. Many times women feel that they did something wrong or the fact that their Mr. Wonderful is abandoning them is somehow their fault. Sometimes women feel they should have seen it coming; the signs must have been there. Something you did made him unhappy. Right? Wrong!

When two people meet they are attracted to each other because of their respective physical attributes. Just think about it. If you are in a crowd and some Prince Charming comes over to chat, what initial information did he have to propel him in your direction? If he was not terribly nearsighted, it had to be your physical attributes. It was all he had to go on at that moment. Perhaps it was the color of your hair, your figure or your smile. Whatever it was, it was physical.

Conversely, you must have felt similarly when he approached you. Good manners in social situations account for a lot, but when it got right down to it you were either pleased with what Mr. Wonderful offered in the way of good looks, a smile or some other physical attribute. Glib conversation and intellect came later as you got to know him -- or at least thought you did.

Once you and Mr. Wonderful decided you wanted to pursue continued interaction, at whatever level, you probably went through a process of identifying mutual interests, friends, culinary likes and dislikes, favorite wines and so forth. You likely shared your lives' histories (with a few tactful omissions) and family stories. The point is you worked at "finding" each other and at approaching a union, assuming you liked what you discovered along the way. This was your courting period. Everyone is at their best while courting. They strive to put their best foot forward overlooking the little things.

When you decided to get married you entered another period of initial accommodation. You were living with another person, perhaps for the first time. He had things he was used to like pressed bed linens or undershorts. After all, his mother had spoiled him that way! You on the other hand were used to meals being served on time and weekends and holidays being planned to get the most out of them. Whatever it was that both of you were "used to", now you had to accommodate each other in some way.

It is likely as the wife and a product of the '50s or '60s that you did the lion's share of the accommodating. It might even have become a pattern. But you did it out of love and to benefit domestic tranquillity. Or at least that's what you told yourself. And in reality it was true. You saw your life being spent with this man and making a nice home in which you both would raise your children. He went to work and provided for the family. It was The American Dream.

Don't look back over the decades and think you should have known better. One woman had this feeling and after careful questioning realized that she, just like you, probably was working with the best information she had at the time. Her Mr. Wonderful had been physically attractive, seemed nice, was from a respected and prosperous community-minded family, wanted children, had a good job -- all the "qualifications" of the proverbial "good catch". As the years went by things changed a bit here and there and she accommodated them because she felt they were marching to the same band.

Always remember that the divorce is not your fault. He initiated it. Don't blame yourself for not seeing the signs of it coming. Understand that your present circumstances are just that -- live in the present. The blame is his -- not yours!

Now that that's settled, let's move along with how to deal with this mess!

4. ADOPTING A "WINNING" ATTITUDE

In sports we hear a lot about the *winning attitude* which implies that in order to have a winner, there has to be a loser. That might work well on the football field or the tennis court, but in the course of human events it seldom is truly successful.

No One Ever Wins in Divorce

It is hoped that one of the effects of this book will be to discourage divorce. If discontented spouses would look beyond their immediate discontent and truly consider the results of divorce, they would probably never undertake it. The literature is rife with statistical and anecdotal evidence that divorce is never beneficial, with perhaps the exception of abusive relationships and lawlessness. But even when divorce is necessary, it damages the participants.

In divorce, a "winning attitude" is a misnomer. The very nature of divorce usually means that there is no winner. All parties lose something. At least one spouse, usually the wife, loses a mate and she never wanted the divorce in the first place. Conversely, often her exiting hubby realizes too late that what he thought he wanted is different from what he got. The grass may not prove to be greener in the other yard. The result is one has been left and one has left and can't return. The children, grandparents, friends and everyone else are caught in the middle of a bad situation.

The children, if there are any, lose at least one parent in the process and maybe two. Young children often won't understand what is going on and why Daddy no longer lives with them. Research indicates that young children often blame themselves for the divorce. One child asked if it was because she didn't clean her room as often as requested.

Adult children suffer too. For years they have looked to both parents for guidance and support. In one case, a married daughter had kept her maiden name in her profession and, following the divorce of her parents, felt ashamed to bear her father's name but had little recourse as that was how she was known professionally.

When the parental union is severed it creates ripples in everyone's life. Recent research has suggested that there is a correlation between out-of-wedlock pregnancies in adult daughters and suicides in adult sons of divorce.

Grandparents lose, too. If they are your husband's parents they often are guilty by association and reap the same or similar treatment as their son. They probably won't be able to see the grandkids as much, if not due to court action, because they feel guilty or embarrassed. It is difficult for them. They are not responsible for their son's actions but are often perceived as his greatest supporters -- and, in fact, may act that way. Conversely, the wife's parents lose much like she does. While feeling the hurt for their daughter, they'll have to confront questions from the grandkids and often they are the people who the rest of the family turn to for support, leadership and comfort. It can be lonely as the only senior members left!

If the divorcing couple are grandparents themselves (which is not as uncommon as you might have thought), the matter is complicated by the fact their grandchildren will be asking their parents what is going on while the parents (children of the divorcing grandparents) are trying to deal with their own pain. The trauma truly becomes intergenerational. Going home to Granny's for the holidays can take on a whole new meaning!

Divorce can be a financial disaster. The process is expensive and the result is that when it's all over two households are financed by the same income, which means everyone feels the pinch. The exception, of course, are the divorces involving very large property settlements. Even then, there can be a financial burden as properties may not be liquid assets.

Well, if no one is a winner, how can you develop a "winning attitude"?

Take the High Road
One of the least positive things you can do for yourself is to speak ill of your Mr. Wonderful. That's not to say you shouldn't be accurate about the issues, but try to be dispassionate in their representation as well. Try to view him as the opposition, nothing more, nothing less.

Speaking ill of your children's father serves no purpose but can have three results. First, it reduces the divorce to a "cat calling competition" which is at best not productive and probably counterproductive. Second, it forces family and friends to take sides. Third, it is probably not true -- everyone has some good attributes about them -- yes, even that nasty fellow who got you into all this! For example, one reported lousy husband was credited with being a wonderful father and grandfather and his children had to admit as much when their mother reminded them of this fact.

In taking the high road you should recognize the positive as well as the negative for what they are -- give the devil his due!

Kill Them With Kindness
We've all heard the adage, "You catch more flies with honey than you do with vinegar." Well, there is a certain amount of truth to that.

If you accept that there is some good in your husband, then it might be very disarming to make it known when the appropriate opportunity occurs at family-wide functions like birthdays, reunions, weddings, funerals and the like. In fact if you are the hostess, be sure you invite him, but also be sure enough other people are there so you won't be too aware of his presence! One ex-wife found this very useful in that it put attendees at ease because they saw she was at ease and they could more aptly deal with the festivities at hand.

Alternative Perspectives -- Think Logic

You need to develop some alternative perspectives about your newly found, if unwanted, situation. The key to those new alternative perspectives can be found in logic. One of the purposes of *Beat Him At His Own Divorce!* is to help you appreciate the value of logic and how it can be applied to make your life a bit more comfortable in a bad time.

With logic there is reason and with reason there is the reality that you are striving for something that will be the best for you and those you love -- not the worst for your departing spouse. In other words, accentuate the positive and try to suppress your desires of "getting even".

There are some techniques for seeking alternative perspectives and infusing logic into this crazy life you have begun so unexpectantly. You might try to look at divorce as a breakup of a partnership, like in a family business. You and your husband are partners and he has decided not to participate in the business any longer. Now the partners have to make an equitable dissolution of the property and responsibilities of the business. As one partner you will "win" if you are able to negotiate a settlement that works for both partners and is practical.

Another way to look at the divorce is to consider how it changes your life and see if there are any new aspects of it that you find pleasing -- you read it right, p-l-e-a-s-i-n-g!

With every change new doors of opportunity are opened. For example, if your husband used to place demands on your time, you might like the idea of having more time to yourself. Or, if there were things you always liked to do but he wasn't too interested in joining you, find someone else who shares that interest and go for it! Other little things in which you might find new liberty could include deciding: what to eat for dinner or where to go if you like eating out, or who gets the shower first, or staying up later or getting up earlier. Every marriage is a compromise of sorts.

Without him in the picture, as well as your bed, you may find new opportunities that make your life more enjoyable. One abandoned wife, found she no longer had to tread softly at night fearful of awakening her light-sleeping husband. For years she had been tippy-toeing around him so as not to disturb his rest and bear the grumpy results if she did.

Whatever it is, with all divorces come changes. Sure they are new and with newness comes uncertainty, but the longer you experience them, the less uncertain and more comfortable they become.

5. DEVELOP A PROJECT PERSPECTIVE

It will help you immensely if you can de-personify the divorce. Admittedly, this is difficult. Try to develop a *project perspective.* That means looking at the divorce like it is a project that will be over in a relatively short period of time when compared with the rest of your life. It will probably seem at times that it will never end and, in fact, some divorces take years. But in reality when it's over you will go on living your life and with time things will get better.

Have you ever heard the expression, "Time is a great anesthesia"? It's true. Think about other losses that people have in their lives -- death of a loved one, financial problems, illness -- with time they are usually resolved and the same will be true of your divorce.

Every project, whether starting a new business, planting a garden and even completing a divorce, has some common characteristics. You can employ them to help you develop a project perspective:

- set a goal for yourself -- decide what you want to get out of the divorce

- determine the information you will need and where to get it

- develop a work plan for finding the information complete with a schedule and assignments

- devise creative ways of working, such as sending copies of selected correspondence from your husband, with your response to children and his relatives and friends to be certain the record is accurate and there is correct communication

- be certain that each work activity is useful and provides a specific product or result so you aren't spinning your wheels

- periodically revise your work plan and evaluate its productivity.

Each one of these characteristics is described in greater detail with examples further in this book.

6. SETTING YOUR GOALS

The simplest way to set your goals is to think, "What's best for me?" Initially you will probably be answering "How 'bout no divorce!?!" But do you really want him back? Some women feel if they are nice and try to be the little understanding wife (probably a role with which they are all too familiar after decades of pleasing Mr. Wonderful!) that he'll see the error of his ways and come home. Forget it! Besides, by now he's probably "used goods" anyway.

So how do you determine what is best for you? This might take some time and it certainly deserves careful thought. It is also a good topic for you to address with your Project Manager. Understand that your goals might change with time and circumstances so be prepared to be flexible.

The following are some examples of goals you may wish to use to stimulate your thinking.

Examples of Goals
The following goal statements evolved during actual divorces. Everyone's situation is different and yet there are many similarities. In many ways, setting these goals can be the beginning of your new life, because they can establish the parameters that will help protect you in later years and to that end there are many types of goals that you might wish to consider. Some are more immediate and related to the divorce and others are more long-term and directed toward improving the quality of life. See what you think:

- To receive ___ % of the property owned in the marriage.

- To have shared custody of the children and ensure them access to both parents as often as they wish.

- To receive a monthly spousal support payment of $ _____.

- To receive a monthly child support payment of $ _____.

- To prevent him from being alone with the children (in abusive situations) except in supervised settings.

- To solely own the house and all the household items in it.

- To obtain ___% of the family business.

- To make time to pursue a college degree, take dancing lessons, travel, or some other activities.

- To stay in touch (or not) with his parents and to encourage the children to do so (or not).

- To not jump into marriage with the next eligible member of the male species to come along.

- To never see the bum again in this life!

The trick is setting goals that are realistic and achievable. You can always change them if needed. But if you don't set them, you will flounder and react to what he and his lawyer offer rather than having a logic of your own for what you want. In setting your goals try to be "fair" (whatever that is!) and make them affordable for Mr. Wonderful. Half of everything is a good place to start!

Sometimes it is good to develop several goals so you have fallback positions if you need them. This can simply be filling in the blanks with different numbers but it can also be quite involved with different scenarios, particularly if there is a lot of property. You will need to present your most desired goal first followed by the lesser desired ones. But don't "goal" him to death!

One wife could never bring herself to define her goals and she didn't take charge of her divorce preferring to turn it over to her attorney. She had trouble dealing with the concept of the whole unpleasant business. The result was her wealthy husband and his high-powered lawyers walked all over her. Her final settlement became a bitter pill that she will have to take every day. She can only blame herself.

Establishing Goals

There are several techniques you can employ to establish your goal(s). One is to work closely with your Project Manager and discuss what it is you want. If he is doing his job, he will ask you some very pointed questions and help you delineate exactly what you want and what you think is reasonable.

Another technique is from the business world and is used to develop a consensus from a group of diverse people about a controversial subject. Take a legal pad of paper and make two lists. The first you can title, "Everything I Want" and the other "Everything I Don't Want". Take your time. Don't rush through it.

Once you have completed the lists discuss them with your Project Manager. Cross off the ones you collectively think should be reconsidered. Add some as they come up and which you might not have thought of during the first writing. When you think you are finished, circle the similar items and group them into clusters. Evaluate the clusters and see what results. Then decide which are the most and least important and write them on a sheet of paper for subsequent referral.

7. DETERMINE YOUR INFORMATION NEEDS

Knowledge is power! Don't forget it.

Gathering information is a very important and time consuming activity during a divorce. It can also be an extremely difficult undertaking, especially in a very contentious or at least difficult divorce.

Inventorying Property
There are several varieties of information that you will need to obtain for your subsequent analysis. Some information is probably at your fingertips and fairly easy to gather. For example, if you are anticipating monthly spousal support, you will need to inventory those costs so you will know how much to seek.

Appendix A contains a sample expense form for doing so. You will need to inventory items such as: cash, financial instruments, household items, bank accounts, insurance policies, real estate, business holdings and tax returns. Appendix B contains a summary property inventory form to assist you in your initial work. You will probably want to add to it your own notes and ideas.

Valuing Property
This can be tricky. Value is somewhat like beauty; it's in the eyes of the beholder. On top of that, both sides will be posturing their view of the property on the balance sheet in hopes of more favorably affecting the bottomline.

In most divorces the husband will be the paying spouse and consequently it is in his interests to devalue the property to reduce the amount to be shared. You must be certain you know what the market value is and there are specialists who can help you. If the divorce is filed in a community property state, he might try to inflate the value of your "half" and devalue that of his to receive a better settlement.

Money and its equivalent is easy to value -- just count it! But properties and business holdings require professional valuation assistance. If there are considerable holdings, the valuation process will be lengthy and costly. Be prepared to spend both time and money on this because if you don't you may regret your final settlement for the rest of your life.

If a business is involved, contact a business appraiser and have him/her tell you its worth. Usually they will give you a low, medium and high value based on the information you can give them about the business. This information might be difficult to obtain from the owners if your husband has partners, but you will need it so the business appraisers can do their job.

If the property is real estate, all you will need is the correct title description and the appraisers can visit the property. However, some site inspection of buildings should be expected for which you will need to gain access. Don't expect an exact figure because there are often special circumstances or factors which will affect the final price.

A common factor in assessing the value of a business is the amount assigned to goodwill. While inventory and equipment can be quantified, goodwill is an intangible that is assigned to the presence of the business in its particular market and how likely (the goodwill) customers are to continue to seek out the goods or services that the business generates.

Business valuations can be difficult and should be undertaken as soon as possible. One woman thought she could at least rely on her half of their jointly owned business to support her financially. Unfortunately, she learned too late that her husband had set up a mirror business with his new girlfriend, diverted clients to that company and all that remained for the wife he left was an empty shell.

Other Information Needs

The nature of your other information needs will be determined by the characteristics of his divorce. For example, if you do not know your husband's annual income you will need to investigate that. Or, if you have not been privy to insurance policies, safety deposit boxes and the like, you will need to find out where they are and their value.

Remember in every divorce one person (often the male) wants to leave and has had the opportunity to plan his exit. Meanwhile his leaving has likely caught you off guard, but he may have been hiding things for a long time. You may wish to commission a "forensic accountant", one who seeks out hidden assets. These people work like a private investigator specializing in how to uncover secret accounts, property holdings and funds that have been laundered with friends and relatives. One woman learned that the "love of her life" had purchased a $400,000 home in which to live with his 22 year old "trophy-wife-to-be" whom he had impregnated, while pleading poverty. That fact gave her considerable leverage before the court and made the cost of the forensic accountant well worthwhile.

Information Inventory

An information inventory is a helpful tool -- and almost a necessity if there is a great deal of information and several people helping you put it together. The inventory will help you keep everything in place and be a constant reminder to you and your advisors of what you have gathered. It will also help you access it quickly when the time comes.

The inventory is a simple list that details the specific documents you have, dates of the information, dates of acquisition, the source, possible uses and to whom it was distributed. If your situation involves a great deal of assets or many sources of information, your inventory might take on the physical characteristics of a file cabinet with an inventory describing the content of each file and a summary of all files in each drawer. Be sure to keep the inventory current and available to your advisors.

The Chronology

At some point or another, you will need to provide chronological information to someone whether it's your attorney or his attorney, accountants, family members, friends or some other relevant party. As time goes by this becomes more difficult because of everything that happens and the ease with which some things can be forgotten. You should religiously keep a log or a diary of daily events. This doesn't mean every trip to the potty or the refrigerator, but significant conversations, events, ideas and such should be included.

One woman used her chronology to provide critical records about the events of her husband's infidelity which resulted in a pregnancy. This changed the judge's ruling about the time that would be permitted to introduce significant information.

Your chronology could prove to be a wonderful asset as it is unlikely the opposition will maintain a log. People doing the wrong thing don't usually like to record it. Remember -- Knowledge Is Power!

Start a File

You will find it useful to keep a file or a series of files with all the information that develops pertinent to the divorce. This may sound rather obvious, but if you don't get organized quickly the influx of information and materials will become overwhelming.

One woman used the occasion of her divorce to establish a formal office in her home from which she would later operate a real estate management business. After the divorce she just emptied the drawers and boxed it up and reorganized her office as a new business managing the properties she secured during the settlement.

8. *ORGANIZING YOUR WORK -- THE TASK PLAN*

Divorces can become very complex projects. The complexity pretty much results from how much information you need to be gathering. But even in the less complicated divorces you still need to have some way to organize your work into a logical order of events to ensure nothing is overlooked. There is a very good and proven management technique you can use called the task plan. This chapter may seem a bit dry and "businessy" but bear with it because learning these lessons can greatly simplify your work later!

There are four elements to a task plan including:

- tasks or statements of activities to be conducted

- a schedule for their completion

- specific products or results that are expected from each task

- assignments of specific people to perform the work.

Appendix C contains a form you can use to develop your own task plan. Simply copy the form for as many tasks as you think you will have and complete the form. If you need more room, copy the form on a legal pad and fill it in.

Tasks

Probably the first task you will confront is to determine in which jurisdiction the divorce will take place. This should be obvious. If you both live in the same state or you both have legal residence in another, then that state probably will be the venue for the case. If you and your husband have legal residence in two different jurisdictions, the issue will need to be resolved. Once jurisdiction is established you need to learn all you can about the rules, regulations and process of divorce in that jurisdiction. Find the answers to questions like:

- What are the grounds for divorce?

- Is it a community property state?

- What are the key filing dates in the divorce process?

- When does the property settlement need to be drafted?

- Are parenting plans required for custody of the children?

- What is required of your attorney and what should you expect him/her to do?

- How is custody of the children usually handled?

Tasks are specific work activities whose completion results in a project being achieved. By determining what has to be done and thinking it through, you can better organize what you need to be doing. At any time you may revise the task plan given new information and challenges that arise.

Developing a task plan takes a little practice but it's worth it because it can keep you organized when your world seems to be going crazy. The following examples of how to do this might be helpful:

Task	Schedule	Assignment
1 -- Inventory Household Items	Month 1	Me
2 -- Determine Monthly Living Expenses	Month 1	Me

3 -- Select a Lawyer

3.1 -- Research Local Bar Association	Month 1/Week1	Me
3.2 -- Obtain Referrals from Friends	Month 1/Week 1	Me
3.3 -- Develop Interview Questionnaire	Month 1/Week 1	Me & PM
3.4 -- Interview Candidate Lawyers	Month 1/Week 2	Me
3.5 -- Review Interview Results	Month 1/Week 3	Me & PM
3.6 -- Select and Retain Lawyer	Month 1/Week 4	Me

4 -- Research and Study Divorce Books	Month 2	Me

[Note: "Me" is you and "PM" is your Project Manager.]

The preceding examples are just that. They may or may not apply to your situation, but they offer an idea about how you can develop the task plan. Working with your Project Manager, you can complete the form in Appendix C. Remember, the task plan is a flexible tool. You will need to change it from time to time to reflect new developments or to accommodate crazy new twists that Mr. Wonderful and/or his attorney have devised.

Scheduling/Products/Assignments

There are two elements to scheduling. The first is sequencing the work to be done to be sure that it occurs in an orderly manner.

The second is to provide you with a deadline to be certain what needs to get done, does. Sometimes the scheduling will be dictated by external forces such as specific filing dates or response dates to Mr. Wonderful's mischievous activities. But try as much as you can to be in charge of your own scheduling. It is often easier to be proactive than responsive to another's requirements.

Every task should have a specific product or result. If it doesn't, you might want to reconsider doing it as it could be a waste of time. In the preceding example the products include:

- an inventory of household goods (Task 1)
- a monthly budget (Task 2)
- a retained lawyer (Task 3)
- a new addition (however, unwanted the books may be!) to your home library (Task 4).

Personnel assignments help keep straight who is doing what. They also help you establish your expectations with your Project Manager and professional advisors such as your attorney and accountant.

Great Dust Collectors

Plans make some of the finest dust collectors in the world! You can take pains to prepare the finest plan possible. But if it isn't implemented and followed and periodically modified, all you have is nothing more than a wonderful dust collector!

Get with your Project Manager and implement the plan. But don't let it get in your way either. It should provide direction and order during a time of chaos and emotional upheaval. Change it if you need to and make it work for you.

9. USING EXTERNAL ASSISTANCE

You didn't ask for it, but now you have it! The simple fact is that in America you cannot go through the divorce system without professional assistance. Lawyers and accountants initially come to mind as being the most obvious professionals most people rely on. Depending on your situation you might also need the services of business evaluators, real estate appraisers, psychotherapists, spiritual leaders or art or jewelry appraisers/dealers, to name a few. Don't hesitate to seek professional assistance when you need it. But select these people well and manage them carefully to keep the costs down.

A word of warning is appropriate now. After having selected a professional to assist you *DON'T*, repeat *DON'T* simply throw up your hands and just turn over everything for him/her to do. This often happens when hiring a lawyer and it may be tempting to do so, but you are the one who has to live with the outcome of his/her work so *you* have to be in charge.

Let's Get This Out of the Way Early...
Often divorcing parties begin by deciding they will use the same lawyer. You may recall from your religious classes that "A man cannot serve two masters." This is very true. How can you expect to have your best interests cared for by the same person who is looking after Mr. Wonderful's? Don't even consider using the same attorney or accountant as the person who has just abandoned you. Get your own from the beginning and be certain he/she is not an acquaintance of either of you.

One woman considered sharing a lawyer but fortunately fought the urge. Not only was the lawyer more interested in her prominent husband's situation than hers, but he proved to be an incompetent and his work products (proposed settlements and other documents) were vague, poorly written and very one-sided. She received a much better settlement thanks to the fastidious investigative work of her own lawyer and accountant.

Selecting External Assistance

One of the most difficult management functions is selecting the right person for the job. In business this is observed routinely. But how do you find the right person such as the lawyer who will represent you?

After you develop your short list from referrals and other sources you need to interview each one. Develop a standard list of questions about how they handle divorces, information about your situation you think they should have, and any other questions that will give you an idea of how you will enjoy working with him/her. Expect to answer questions your candidates may have for you, too. Professionals worth their salt will want to see if you and your situation are worth their time and effort. The results of the interviews should give you some good insights.

Some people call it "intuition", for others it's a "sixth sense" or "gut instinct". Whatever it's labeled, don't dismiss it. Recent studies have demonstrated that victims of crimes in large cities often disregard their sixth sense and that's what gets them into trouble. Apparently there is something "numbing" about large cities. Don't let this divorce mess numb you too! If the professional you are interviewing doesn't "feel right" then he or she may not be the right person for you. On the other hand, if you are offered a complimentary copy of this book, you're probably on the right track!

Remember the professionals you will interview are in business. Their business is one of problem solving and you need to be sure that they will represent you in a manner consistent with your desires, philosophies and belief system. You will be relying on their expertise, but they still work for you. Be sure to obtain and check their client references. Obviously, they will only provide names of people satisfied with their services, but check them out anyway -- you never know what you might learn.

Understand Their Business Practices Up Front

A wise person once said, "Don't pay early and don't pay late, just pay on time." The last thing you need is a disgruntled member of your team. Find out how they like to be paid, what their business practices are and if you agree with them, comply. If you don't, then negotiate another arrangement or select another appropriate person.

It's difficult to know exactly how much professional services in a divorce will cost. But ask for their rates and get them to give you a best and worst case range of total costs. If they are reluctant to provide it, don't be put off. Look for a compromise. If money is tight, discuss how you might be able to reduce the bill by doing some of the work yourself.

Sometimes the less professional tasks they assign to their personnel are something you can do as well. However, if you've hired the head of the firm, don't agree to be shuffled off to less expensive staff unless they're good and it's agreed you are paying for their time at their rates. Know what and whom you are buying!

There are some new developments in the practice of divorce law, it appears. A recent article by Dion Haynes in the *Chicago Tribune* entitled *Lawyers Untangle Legal Morass with Client-Friendly Advice* (October 26, 1997) reported an emerging trend that may be of interest to you.

Apparently, the legal profession is realizing that people want more control over their situations and some lawyers are serving as "legal consultants" and unbundling divorce legal services to meet their clients' needs. Traditionally, people select a lawyer to handle their divorce and are charged a price for doing so. Now, however, some lawyers are serving as consultants who will review what you do or write for a much lower fee. For example, if a letter needs to be written it might cost $1000 to have the lawyer do it. But if you are reasonably competent in that department, you may be able to write it and pay as little as $100 or $200 for your lawyer to review it.

The trend is becoming so popular (and coupled with the negative views of attorneys -- we've all heard the jokes) that the American Bar Association is studying the positive effects of such unbundled services on the legal profession. It's definitely something to consider!

When you have gathered all of the information that you can, meet with your Project Manager and discuss what you've learned, including your intuition about the candidates. Then make your selection.

Taking Charge
The entire premise of this book is that *you* will take an active role in managing your response to Mr. Wonderful divorcing you. If you are not prepared to do this, kindly close the book now and give it to some other deserted woman who might benefit from it and has the gumption to use it. If you are prepared to take charge, reinforce your commitment now by reciting:

"I MUST TAKE CHARGE OF HIS DIVORCE!!"

Say it again, *"I MUST TAKE CHARGE OF HIS DIVORCE!!"*

And again, *"I MUST TAKE CHARGE OF HIS DIVORCE!!"*

Now let's talk about managing the professionals who will make up your team.

The first thing you need to do is clearly establish a team leader who will be coordinating everyone's work on your behalf. That will probably be the lawyer you select. Or, you might serve as the coordinator and keep all of the team members informed about the overall progress and any needs that will crop up.

Teddy Roosevelt had a wonderful observation, "When you hire people, have the good sense to get the best and the better sense to let them do their work." The point is you can't micro-manage people and expect good results. Rather, give them direction and then rely on their expertise to do their work and give you results. If you don't get the result you want, fire them and get some new blood on the team.

One woman went through three lawyers before she got the results she wanted. In her case she was seeking reasonable communication, correct billings and generally "a little respect". It took three attorneys before she found the right one.

The key to good personnel management is good communications and making decisions at the lowest level of authority. That means you should talk to your professionals frequently, keep current with the progress of their work and rely on their judgment to make routine professional decisions. Don't require them to check everything with you before making a decision. Don't become the bottleneck in the decision making.

Provide general direction and respond promptly to their questions and make your policy decisions clear. As the team works together a certain "rhythm" should develop that will help you in your management role. Also, your Project Manager can "look over your shoulder" and offer advice to keep you on track.

"Introduce" Them to Mr. Wonderful
Much of the divorce process is anticipation of how the opposition will react to proposals and positions your side will take. Understanding the personality, attributes, habits and weaknesses of the opposition -- your Mr. Wonderful -- can go a long way to helping you *Beat Him at His Own Divorce!* So take the time to acquaint your pro-

fessional advisers as well as your Project Manager with how the man you slept with all those years thinks. After all, no one knows him better than you.

One wife had professional as well as personal knowledge of her Mr. Wonderful. You see, during all those years of being "his lovely wife" she also earned a graduate degree in psychology and developed a psychotherapy practice. She had difficulty understanding his actions in seeking the divorce and took the time to clinically evaluate him. The result was that he suffered from narcissistic personality disorder, big time!

With that understanding she described the personality disorder in layman's terms to her Project Manger, lawyer, forensic accountant and real-estate appraiser. The whole focus of the settlement became one of how to make him feel he looked good being "fair" to her. It worked! Her eventual settlement was considerably larger than what his side originally proposed.

Another client realized that her Mr. Wonderful's Achilles heel was a small southern farm among rolling hills and the image of the landed gentry. She explained that to her team and they constructed a plan that helped her leverage that desire to her best interests.

10. MAINTAINING YOUR RESOLVE

One of the most difficult attributes to muster during a divorce is resolve. Your opposition will be resolved because it is of his making; he has new goals that he wants to achieve and they don't include you. There will be times when you sicken of the whole mess and it seems as though he is unbeatable. You may be tempted to throw in the towel and let him dictate the terms of the final settlement.

DON'T DO IT!

If you do, you will be giving up "long-term gain for short-term pain". In other words, because you don't want to deal with the problem at the time and are willing to take whatever you get, you will have to live with whatever the settlement decision becomes. It is better by far to put up with whatever difficulties there are in the short-term to achieve the settlement you will be living with the rest of your life. The difficulties of the divorce process will fade, but a bad settlement will be a constant reminder of your weakness.

People have different ways of staying "up" when times are tough. Whatever yours are, you'll need them now! However, if you find yours aren't serving you very successfully, here are a few ideas that may bolster you.

Don't Dwell on Your Problems
This is hard to do. Divorce magnifies everyday problems because half your support system is gone. That guy you counted on and looked up to is now the cause of your aggravation, self-doubt and torment, not the resource of comfort he used to be. Whatever your views were about "hearth and home", they have been altered and you simply have to accept that as your new reality.

At times you will have sinking spells when you start remembering some of the good times. You also will worry about what the future brings. You may begin doubting what you are doing. Or, you may tire of the whole process -- the continual strain that comes with trying to find information that will help your side or the effect the whole mess has on your family and friends. Accept the situation as being one not of your doing and work through it.

Ask yourself, "Do I really want him back?" What if he did come back? Would things be the same as they were -- hardly. Here's an easy measure -- do you really want to share his bed again? Even if you fooled yourself by answering "yes" to these questions, you'd soon learn that "no" was the inevitable response because it wouldn't be long before the hard memories and harsh words of near divorce would teach you that lesson. These are difficult things to overcome. No, you're now probably on a one-way road from which any deviation will produce less than the hoped for results.

Let Others Help You
The concept of having a Project Manager and other experts was discussed earlier. Don't relinquish your role in managing their activities on your behalf, but do take advantage of them shouldering some of the emotional strain. They can do this by helping you with such tasks as sorting through old records and any belongings he left behind and reviewing relevant correspondence and pictures. Their participation will reduce your likelihood of dwelling in the past and becoming self-absorbed in your problems.

Keep Laughing
Whenever you can, look for the humor in what you are doing. That might now sound crazy, especially if you are just beginning the divorce process and feeling completely put upon by it and him. But the fact is you will come to see humorous elements in it.

You may recall idiosyncrasies of Mr. Wonderful that you no longer have to endure. Or, you may be able to second-guess some response your almost "ex" will make to your lawyer's negotiations that are predictable based on some traits you know about him.

One ex-wife marveled at how she no longer had to have the master's dinner ready each night, not knowing until the last minute whether or not he was coming home. Since there wasn't anyone to cook for, she found she enjoyed eating out frequently each week with friends and family, or not eating at all if she wasn't hungry!

It is critical that you maintain your resolve to complete the task plan you have prepared. You will have to be on top of everything at once and you will need to do all the other things that went on in your life before you were thrown into the whole divorce mess. However, you can take some solace in the fact that others have done it before you and there are people who can help you -- and, most importantly, *it will be over some day and some day will take less time than the rest of your life!!!!*

11. BE CREATIVE

Divorces are not the most creative uses of human resources. While they can be deadly dull at times, they can also be very exciting if not hostile affairs. With all the fighting and positioning, conversations between lawyers, advice from well-meaning friends and relatives, information gathering and uncertainties, you will need to find ways to work creatively. Also, the process can dictate how you work and you have to be careful of that.

If one of your external professionals tells you something can't be done (just because it never was before) and you think it should be done -- question it and do it! Remember the anecdote about the woman whose attorney didn't want her to address the court? She felt she should because the attorney was not making an effort to tell the judge about her Mr. Wonderful's love child. She spoke up and changed things for the better for herself in spite of her attorney's wishes.

Here are some suggestions to get you thinking about creative work habits.

Circulate Information
Often in a divorce, the other side will start spreading half truths of what is transpiring to look good to family and friends. You have to get your message and relevant information out.

One woman received handwritten letters from her Mr. Wonderful. She decided to forward them to their children, his parents and siblings. She also copied them on her responses. He was mortified! He thought he could cower her and that she would keep the communication private between them leaving him to tell others what he wanted them to hear. He looked quite silly when the two letters arrived together and other family members could read them for themselves. It was a wonderful tactic!

Start a Newsletter
This may sound real silly but it does provide an outlet as well as the ability to send a subtle message that you are in charge. People will want to know how you are doing and yet they will be afraid to ask because you might tell them more than they really want to know. So start a monthly, bi-monthly or quarterly newsletter.

Don't address the divorce directly, you don't want folks to think you are broadcasting your hurt. Rather let everyone know how well you are doing. Give them updates about your job, talk about the children or grandchildren, send them seasonal wishes or ideas. By conspicuously not mentioning Mr. Wonderful or his divorce they will get the message. Besides it will be fun to demonstrate that for you, life can go on without him.

You may be surprised at their reactions -- many will write you back with "atta girl" cards or invitations to social events. Many will tell you how much they like the idea. You and everyone, except Mr. Wonderful, will enjoy it. It also gives you a sense of future and the more pleasant side of life.

Production of the newsletter is not difficult with today's computer programs. But even if you hand write it neatly and have it copied at the local printer, it provides you with an excellent vehicle to stay in touch. You might include favorite recipes, holiday stories, a few jokes or thoughts about issues (non-divorce ones!) of the day.

Helping Him with His Divorce
You read the subtitle correctly. Sometimes you have to help the competition to get what you want! That may sound bizarre but given the fact you don't want him back, you may as well get on with your new life and you can't do that until the divorce is final.

The final settlement, the one you have to live with, will be a function of the negotiation process between your side and his. Sometimes you have to show the opposition how they can get what they want by giving you what you want. Remember, they probably aren't very creative so you have to be.

One woman ran into this in a very large property settlement situation. Her experts soon knew more about the jointly-owned property than the opposition did. She was able to offer several scenarios with different combinations of properties that would achieve the settlement. But she had to do the research for them and couldn't rely on their understanding of the situation. A good rule of thumb is to treat the settlement process as a problem solving one rather than simply one demand after another.

As you create his solutions, you might be on the look out for little leverage points. One woman's attorney was reviewing documents and found an "irregular" signature on a deed that was supposed to be that of her client. It was clearly a forgery that had been made many years before. Now wouldn't that look good before a judge if a settlement couldn't have been achieved?!?

Knowledge is power and you can negotiate in a more powerful manner if you have one or two "aces" up your sleeve, whether or not you decide to play them.

Use Your Investigative Experts

In Chapter 9, the concept of retaining external experts was discussed. Now is the time to use them. When large estates are involved in the settlement dispute, it is likely that you will have problems finding everything. If he has been planning his departure for some time he may have secreted resources in foreign banks, silent partnerships or with friendly family members.

will find more than he intends for you to find and it will improve your settlement. If possible, provide your accountant with the Social Security numbers of everyone in the family and other close relatives. Make a list of all the names these people and his friends go by. This may permit identification of joint accounts or recently created companies.

Cash can be very difficult to find since it can be hidden easily if a person has planned to leave for years. Some ways are traveler's checks, savings bonds, giving cash to trusted friends and relatives to hold for later, or even stashing it under a mattress!

Everyone's situation in a divorce is a bit different. As you go through his divorce, you will likely identify some additional opportunities for creativity. Don't pass them up. Your Project Manager might be able to help you come up with some of them as well.

12. SOME NEGOTIATING HINTS

Negotiating a divorce settlement is different than most other forms of negotiations because of the emotional overtones that accompany divorce. There are often feelings of betrayal and revenge. Egos run high. The uncertainty of the future years creates an atmosphere not at all conducive to the negotiation process. However, there are a few things you can do to improve your chances of getting what you want during the settlement.

The First Rule of Negotiation
"Never sit down at a table you can't afford to walk away from" was the advice of George Meany. Now you may or may not be favorably impressed with unions, but one thing they have a lot of experience in is negotiating and Meany was one of the best. His advice is good for you now.

If you feel you simply must win something and are compelled to negotiate no matter what happens, you may have lost before you start. You will need to give something to get something. Negotiation is a compromise. And, it is for the competition too. Try to establish an atmosphere of negotiating in good faith so both sides understand that they are trying to achieve the end product -- the settlement.

Know What You Want
Earlier the subject of what you want was addressed. When you reach the negotiation table you should be in pretty good command of that subject. You will need an "ideal" settlement scenario and a couple of back-up positions. Try to anticipate the opposition's positions and be flexible in case they come up with an approach your team hasn't thought of and might be altered to your benefit.

A good psychological point is to require Mr. Wonderful to make the first offer. Just like you did by having him file for divorce thereby formally being recognized as the offending party, make him play his cards first in the negotiations. You might learn something useful, if only what tactic he will be taking. But don't be surprised if he starts with a low "bid", pretending he is in a weak financial condition.

Develop a Rationale

All of the data gathering and analysis undertaken by your team should give you the information you need to clearly outline for your negotiator what you want to capture during the negotiations. Be organized and have a logic behind each position you take. Remember that simply demanding property and concession is not very impressive and probably won't get you far. Make the opposition focus on the rationale of your negotiation rather than the items it garners.

One woman was being divorced in a community property state and her basic logic was "I get half -- it's the law." Another didn't live in a community property state and she established the "half rationale" by reminding him that everything to date had been a 50/50 deal -- the "I dos", the kids, loans from her family, joint participation in the family business, etc. That worked too.

You need to develop a logic because it will serve to guide him and his negotiators to the end you seek. In sales a common technique is to get the person to make affirmative statements: "Nice weather we're having." "Sure is."; "Are you comfortable in that chair?" "Yes I am."; "Do you want your kids to go to college?" "Yes, I do."... The result is they make little affirmations all along which makes it easier to say "yes" to your points. This has to be done subtly but it is a useful technique.

Get a Negotiator

You cannot effectively negotiate for yourself. There are several reasons for this. First, you need a buffer between you and the opposition. If you were to handle your own negotiation you could be pressured into making on the spot decisions and not given the opportunity to carefully consider your position. A negotiator can always say, "I have to run that by my client".

Another reason for using a negotiator is simply that they are usually more experienced at these things than you are. They have participated in other negotiations, perhaps divorces, and understand the process and various approaches.

Negotiations are best conducted dispassionately. Mr. Wonderful probably knows some terrific ways to get under your skin and irritate you. You don't need that happening during a negotiation. Negotiators can provide you with that protection.

Selecting a Competent Negotiator
You will need to take care in selecting a negotiator. Preferably you want someone who is extremely experienced in such things and is dispassionate about your situation. You want someone who is not acquainted with your almost "ex" husband but does understand how he thinks from your descriptions of him. You want a clear thinker and one who will take his/her marching orders from you but offer suggestions as they might occur. You probably do not want your Project Manager to serve in this capacity because he is your private resource to monitor everyone else's activities on your behalf and give you policy advice about what you should do next.

Your negotiator should be business-like and well focused. He/ She should not be easily intimidated or subject to any position or celebrity that your husband might represent. Also, it is important that your negotiator not work on a contingency. Make arrangements to pay him/her a fee for the service. If it is based on a contingency of what you receive in the settlement, it could influence the negotiation. As with other experts on your team, discuss the candidates with your Project Manager and make a final decision.

Be Reasonable

You need to get the best settlement you can, because you will have to live with it. At the same time you can't be so demanding that the settlement will not be possible. Be reasonable when the opportunity merits it. Remember, everyone needs to feel like a winner to be successful. Equally important though is the fact that you don't have to give away the farm -- or the house, the car, the business...!

The Pivotal Point

Often in negotiations of any kind, there is one issue that becomes the pivotal point -- the critical point that makes or breaks the final agreement. Watch for it. It might be a piece of property, visitation schedule or a family heirloom. If you can anticipate it, so much the better. Be willing to give in on this point and you might get more than you originally thought possible.

One woman knew that a particular piece of real estate was the object of her husband's attention. She constructed four scenarios that revolved around his having that property. He was so focused on his goal that he gave up more than he might have needed.

Select the Setting

Negotiations require careful thought and concentration. Select the setting for yours. If it would be difficult to dictate the setting, at least review it the day before with your negotiator to see if it is acceptable. If it is not comfortable, obtain a change of venue and date. It is important that your team is comfortable and as undistracted as possible from the matters at hand.

Should you even be there? There are two schools of thought on this subject. If you are absent there is a certain psychological advantage to that. Your absence will be noticed which may give you an edge. It also means you have confidence in your negotiator and that confidence can unnerve the competition sometimes. If you are present you can observe what transpires and make confidential comments to your negotiator. But if you do, be sure your negotiator is the only person who speaks for you. *DON'T SPEAK FOR YOURSELF!* You want to keep the opposition at arm's length.

Take Regular Breaks

Thinking is hard work. Take regular breaks during the negotiations. Ten or 15 minutes every hour and a half is not unreasonable. It gives your team a chance to refresh and confer privately. Also, schedule breaks after specific points are reached. It is a good way to bring closure and refocus on the next issue. At any time during the negotiation do not hesitate to call for a break to confer or refresh. There are no "rules" *per se* unless they are agreed to before the negotiations begin.

Don't Send Signals

Nothing is more unnerving to a negotiator than to have his/her client seated in the next chair and reacting to everything that is said so the opposition can see it. Don't send signals to the opposition! If they say something that offends you, let it go. If they do something outrageous, don't show it. If they fall into a trap you have set for them, don't be smug. Don't send signals!

Negotiation is a fine art. There are some things you can do to better equip your team to work on your behalf, but understand that the situation can be very fluid.

13. PROTECTING YOUR SETTLEMENT

The settlement you win is worthless if you are not able to protect it. How many times have you heard of spousal or child support payments not being paid? You can use a variety of financial instruments such as life insurance, annuities, a bank note due payable to you on a certain date and tax-free real estate exchanges to help protect your settlement.

Whatever protection you seek be sure to have your financial, tax and legal advisors review it. Be sure to complete any insurance transactions before the divorce is final because you will not have an "insurable interest" after your "Mrs." designation is revoked. You won't be able to own insurance on Mr. Wonderful unless you owned it before the divorce is final.

Life Insurance to Cover Your Spousal Support
Life insurance can be a very useful tool for you. One strategy is to insure (before the divorce is final) Mr. Wonderful with you as the designated owner of the policy. If he should die the tax-free death benefit would provide you with the support he agreed to pay in the settlement.

Although initially a bit more expensive than term life insurance, whole life is the best bet because the premiums remain level and never go up, the total expenditure in premiums will probably be less than term life would be, it accumulates a cash value on a tax-deferred basis and the death benefit increases over time. In addition, the cash value of the policy can be withdrawn tax-free as a lien against the eventual death benefit (for which there is often an interest charge but that is usually also treated as a lien against the death benefit).

The insurance can also cover your children in the event your "ex" dies. Be sure the policy is large enough to provide both spousal and child support. The cash value in the policy can also be used as a supplemental retirement fund for your later years.

Life Insurance to Protect Your Estate

If there is a large estate involved, you may wish to provide for your share of it through life insurance. By doing this you will not have to deal at the time of his demise with the next lucky lady to marry Mr. Wonderful. Also, you won't have to deal with any of her or their children. Whole life insurance is again the best vehicle for this. As owner, you may designate anyone you wish to be the beneficiary, including yourself.

Life Insurance to Provide for Your Children

One form of protection for your children was discussed in terms of their father being insured with the children as beneficiaries when he dies.

Another form of protection is to purchase the policies on your children themselves with you as the owner so he can't change his mind. In this latter situation, their father agrees to purchase enough insurance to give the children a tax-free supplemental retirement program equal to their portion of the estate which is calculated to their age of retirement. The child is insured and you are the owner. When the child retires he/she can withdraw the cash value, usually tax-free as retirement income. This approach can be less costly to their father. Also, it protects your grandchildren should their parent (your child) die.

Paid-up Insurance Policies

Remember that whole life insurance policies accumulate cash value and dividend growth. If Mr. Wonderful isn't feeling so wonderful and won't make the premium payments, you may arrange with the insurance company to use the dividends in the policy to pay for the premiums after a certain period of time. This usually doesn't occur for 10 to 15 years depending upon the dividends the company pays.

Be sure you select a highly rated company which is strong enough to ensure that the funds will be there when you need them. You can check these ratings by contacting your state insurance commissioner.

Using Annuities for Your Spousal Support

If your spousal support is set for a specific number of years and you do not trust your soon-to-be ex-hubby to pay it, you might consider having him purchase an annuity for you. This is a financial vehicle by which a lump sum of money is deposited with a financial institution such as an insurance company or stock brokerage house. The institution then guarantees payments (monthly, annually, semi-annually or quarterly) to the annuitant (you).

This is a good vehicle because it prevents Mr. Wonderful from being able to withhold monthly spousal payments from you. It also helps him because it requires less total money than all the spousal payments added up over the years. The reason for this is that the annuity earns interest and so the principal grows while the payments are being made. But the disadvantage to your departed spouse is that it requires a lump sum, up front payment that can be very substantial, depending on your settlement and the length of time you will be receiving support. But then, who left who?

Tax-Free Real Estate Exchanges

If the divorce settlement involves a large real estate portfolio, you may wish to look into tax-free real estate exchanges. This is because the property, if purchased many years ago, may have appreciated significantly. So much so, that if you were to liquidate it there could be a substantial tax burden. By exchanging the property with a third party for another piece of property, you may be able to improve your holdings by trading for a piece that can be partially liquidated as you need it without paying the entire taxes at one time.

Tax exchanges are very complex and in keeping with the comments in the *Foreword*, this book does not provide accounting or legal advice. However, you should know these exist and consider learning more about them and how they apply to your particular situation. You might consider "selling" your half interest in a specific piece of property to Mr. Wonderful. Sometimes this will help you get around costly capital gains taxes and worrying about an outside buyer.

A word of caution about real estate holdings: even after the divorce, the lending institutions (the mortgage holder, if there is a mortgage) won't necessarily remove your name from the mortgage. You should require Mr. Wonderful to refinance all property that will remain in his possession in order to have your name removed from the debt. Refinancing is the only way that the lending institutions will permit your name to be removed from the debt. After all, you don't want to be responsible for his debts after the divorce!

Promissory Bank Notes

The cornerstone of one woman's final settlement was a promissory bank note. She required her Mr. Wonderful to take out a loan with a bank, solely in his name, and pay her the amount borrowed as a portion of her settlement. This achieved two objectives. First it got her the money, clean and outright. Second, it made him accountable to a third party, the bank, for its repayment.

Insurance, annuities, promissory bank notes and tax-free real estate exchanges are handy and creative ways to protect you and your children from financial burdens after Mr. Wonderful exits. The major point is you want him legally accountable to another party and to have yourself "cashed out". That way he can't hold future payment compliance over your head like the Sword of Damocles, making you squirm whenever the next installment comes due! You may never really be rid of him, but these techniques will help to minimize future contacts.

14. READY FOR A FEW GIGGLES?

Humor is an important part of life. If we couldn't laugh at ourselves a little we'd probably all go crazy. Well, as important as humor is in the course of human events, it is even more so during a divorce. But you're probably not feeling very mirthful right now. As time progresses you will get your sense of humor back -- really!

Comeuppance Humor

Some humor that you will find in your situation will simply be a result of the actions taken by Mr. Wonderful -- and you won't have had to do a thing! You will come to see that little things will happen that will put a smile on your face and they are things that don't result from anything you have or have not done. For example, one woman reported that her departed husband swore there was no other woman. Not long thereafter, he announced to his adult children that they had a new little brother!

Another ex-wife reported that her outspoken three-year-old grandchild asked her granddaddy over dinner one night why he wasn't living with grandma any more!

A third woman decided she would continue to frequent the same local pub that she always had when she was part of a couple. When she arrived it was obvious that her Mr. Wonderful decided to do the same, except he brought her replacement with him. She walked up and shook hands with her replacement and expressed best wishes for her happiness with him!

There will be a great many such opportunities unless you are separated by many miles, states or countries. It is only logical. Your former husband has initiated a course of action that will eventually prove an embarrassment to him in situations such as the preceding. Keep your eyes and ears open for them and your wits about you so

Keep your eyes and ears open for them and your wits about you so you can take advantage of the situation and enjoy the moments.

Self Humor

Sometimes you will find years of habits are hard to deny. They have an almost embarrassing way of coming up at the damnedest times. Perhaps you find yourself using your former married name when addressing others. Maybe you notice that something you have done for years to please him you are still doing out of habit, like showering at night so he can be first in the morning, or eating meals at precise times and so forth. One woman would run quickly up the stairs. She was used to being softly pinched on the posterior (she had thought lovingly!) by her Mr. Wonderful to get her to move quickly on the stairs in their house!

Stereotypical Humor

There are endless jokes about the age old conflict of spouses and the genders. We've all heard them. As you become further disassociated from Mr. Wonderful, they will once again begin to put a smile on your face. You might even find yourself nodding in agreement when you recognize the speaker's lead-in.

General Humor

You have to laugh. Right now that might seem a distant faded remembrance of how your life was, "once upon a time". But soon you will enjoy a good (or even a bad) joke again. If you need a bit of encouragement to get started, purchase a few tapes that professional comedians make with themes like growing up in the country, dieting, getting along with the in-laws, exercise programs for couch potatoes and so forth. Learn to laugh again!

15. DO YOU REALLY WANT REVENGE?

There is an old adage, "Vengeance is a plate best served cold." What that means in part is that people who you would like to see "get theirs" probably will. By not being personally involved in it, you will be able to enjoy it that much more.

But revenge is a two-edged sword. By seeking it, it can consume you. Many people who plot and scheme another person's demise become obsessed with the plotting and the "chase", as it were. Often when it finally takes place, it isn't nearly as satisfying as they thought it would be. What a let-down for all the effort!

It's better to expend your energies on something positive. Helping others, building a new business or some artistic endeavor is much more satisfying than setting up Mr. Wonderful for a big downfall. Besides, it is much less frustrating and you have something that others can admire when you are done. Wasn't it one of Donald Trump's former wives who said, "The best revenge is living well"? That's good advice.

There is a theory that says, "what goes around, comes around". Often this is true but there are always exceptions. When Mr. Wonderful left you and the kids, he set into motion a series of events which most likely will take on a life of its own. They may even become a trap for him. The dynamics of a divorce and all that it entails, as well as the resulting various changes in relationships, will become beyond his control. An entirely new set of dynamics will evolve. If there isn't a clear "right" and "wrong" in your situation, there probably is a "just desserts" component. Let it all play out by itself. You will be surprised how much better your situation will look after a few years.

One woman did not believe her situation would improve with time, which she uttered through tear stained cheeks. One year later

71

she was reminded of the events the preceding year and had to admit that she was a bit better. The second, third and fourth years on that date she was reminded again of her "loss". She began smiling at the third year and actually laughing by the fourth "anniversary" of his leaving. It does go away!

If you still want revenge you can try to do what a woman in North Carolina did in August of 1997. She sued the second wife, her replacement, for $1,000,000 and won on the grounds that the woman had stolen her husband and broken up the marriage. The jury only deliberated for three hours. It was possible for her because North Carolina is one of 12 states that still permits suing for "alienation of affections". Whether or not she ever gets the money, the decision very publicly identified the second wife as the cause of the divorce. That is not very conducive to domestic harmony when the "newly-weds" set up housekeeping!

You may recall another woman mentioned earlier got a sort of "pre-emptive revenge" by videoing her husband and his new girlfriend in great detail as they frolicked naked in his apartment. She was able to do that because she could put emotion aside and gather the evidence.

16. INSPIRATION

If there is a corollary to not seeking revenge, it is the inspiration that you can take from many sources. Give your spirits a lift. Inspiration can be of a formal religious nature or it can be simply the realization that life is basically good and it was meant to be enjoyed. Divorces like other difficult periods will pass with time. Time is a great anesthesia for these kinds of losses.

Religion and Divorce

Regardless of what religion you practice, there is some form of solace that can be derived from it when you are going through a divorce. If you are particularly religious, the process of religion such as praying, speaking with your religious leaders and attending services can be very comforting. Whether you were raised with *Ave Maria* or *Give Me That Ol' Time Religion,* returning to those roots can be very settling.

Believe it or not you aren't the first person to go through a divorce, and you won't be the last. That may not be much comfort, but it will provide you with some experienced resources that can help you get through it. You might consider making your religious leaders part of your team, but as previously discussed, not the Project Manager.

Non-Religious Support

Whether or not you are religious, you might find comfort in the many support groups that are out there to help people in times of trouble. There are divorce support groups but often they become seances in which everyone tells their story. Too much of this can be depressing.

What you might look for is something that addresses the characteristics of your situation and the concept of divorce itself. If Mr.

Wonderful became compulsive about something before leaving and you suspect that had something to do with why he left, look into organizations such as Al Anon. They deal with addictive behaviors which sometimes manifest themselves in substance abuse.

Compulsive behavior is just that, and the lessons of groups that deal with it might help you. Also, there is no particular doctrine or belief system that you need embrace. Rather there are guidelines that offer much logic such as:

"You are not responsible for anyone other than yourself."

"You can't change anyone but yourself."

"Replace fear with faith."

"You can't change the progression of the disease of discontent."

Try out a few groups and see if they do anything for you. If they don't, move on. If they do, get involved with them to the extent you are comfortable. One woman found that in order to feel better about her problems, she would go volunteer in some capacity helping people who really were in a bad way like the homeless, AIDS babies or the mentally challenged. It did wonders for her and it might do the same for you.

Some Diversionary Thoughts

Inspiration can come from many sources. If you are a strong personality, you might find some of your own just from observing the world around you. Here are a few thoughts from many sectors. Some you might find useful in weathering your storm:

Have you ever noticed how much better you feel after a good night's sleep? Make it a practice not to make any critical decisions until you have had a chance to "sleep on it" as the old admonition goes. It works!

When was the last time you sat up late at night and looked at the moon and stars? The vastness of what you see can help put things in perspective. It's also quite beautiful.

After a thunderstorm, do you remember how new and clean the world seems? Try to envision that on a cool night before you go to bed. If there is a storm coming your way, watch for it and enjoy it.

When was the last time you played with a child or smelled baby powder? Find a friend with a newborn or toddler and spend some time with them. There is a certain freshness and renewal that comes from such visits.

How's your fox-trot? Go dancing with some friends, nothing heavy, just a good time out of the house. The exercise of a fast waltz is healthy for you aerobically and the change of scenery will do you good.

If you like music, listen to it. If you play an instrument, do so an hour or two a day. Better yet, write a song.

There is a lot more to life than what Mr. Wonderful represented. But you need to get back in touch with it. You'll probably discover in retrospect that his presence might have interfered with your interest in some of these things if only because he wasn't interested and you were appeasing him on the matter.

Sayings Worth Remembering
Remember how the idea of having a theme for the settlement negotiation was suggested to help it make sense to the other side? Well, you might want to adopt a theme for your own sanity and peace

of mind. Here are some sayings that can help bolster you during his divorce. Pick a few you like and hang them on your refrigerator or, better yet, make a few up yourself.

"Of all the people you will know in a lifetime, you are the only one you will never leave or lose, therefore, to the question of your own life you are the only solution."

"Marriage is about love and divorce is about money -- the sooner you get this in you head and heart, the better you'll do."

"We are all faced with a series of great opportunities brilliantly disguised as impossible situations!"

"Life isn't fair, but it's good anyway."

"Life is short -- eat dessert first!"

"Wouldn't it be nice if our lives were like VCRs and we could 'fast forward' through the crummy times?"

"What I know is when you bond with a child, you really can't tell where you stop and that child begins."

"If you don't stand for something, you'll fall for anything."

"From birth to 18 a girl needs good parents. From 18 to 35 she needs good looks. From 35 to 55 she needs a good personality. From 55 on, she needs cash!"

"Stress is the confusion created when one's mind overrides the body's basic desire to choke the living s*#! out of some a**h#~! who desperately deserves it!"

"A gem cannot be polished without friction nor people perfected without trials."

"It is only with the heart that one can see rightly; what is essential is invisible to the human eye."

"Even more than the pill, what has liberated women is that they no longer need to depend on men economically."

"If you agree to stop telling lies about me, I promise not to tell the truth about you."

"People who lose their moral compass will remain adrift on the sea of despair."

And the author's personal favorite, "You can fix a lot of things in life, but you can't fix dumb!"

Sayings like these can help you focus yourself. However, they are no substitute for the satisfaction of obtaining the property settlement you deserve and getting on with your life!

17. OF COURSE YOU'RE DYING TO KNOW!

Television and Hollywood play a more extensive role in our lives than we would probably like to admit. They make their revenues based on their reflections of our lives. Consequently, divorce is a very prominent theme in their work because it is so apparent in our lives. Often they depict the emotional and conspiratorial sides of divorce and the people who are thrown into it, complete with private investigators and lots of mystery and intrigue.

Real divorces are not movie material. Rather they are somewhat routine affairs that at least temporarily scramble the lives of all involved. But many do have some Hollywood elements about them. If Mr. Wonderful's divorce is cinemagraphic material, you might be tempted to hire a private investigator to learn everything you can about your departed hubby's activities in hopes that it will help you negotiate a better settlement. *DON'T DO IT!*

Of course you want to know everything he's been up to! You are dying to know if your suspicions about that coworker or the sales convention last year have merit. Or maybe you know who the other person is and your psyche demands the explicit details.

Snooping around is similar to revenge in that it is a two-edged sword that can consume you. And what do you really have when it's all over? Isn't it enough to know you've been abandoned? Why dig up all the dirty details that will only amplify how bad you already feel? Why spend all that time and money on that kind of external assistance when it would be much better spent investigating hidden accounts, unusual expenditures and other things that would help you negotiate your settlement?

On the other hand, don't discard information that is reported to you by friends or relatives. You'll be surprised what you'll learn once people know you have been left. One woman heard from a half dozen sources the name of the other woman whom she had suspected all along. Another discovered from a third-party that she would never be able to compete because her Mr. Wonderful had found a Mr. Wonderful of his own! Additionally, a very successful psychiatrist who co-wrote books on child abuse with his new squeeze turned out to be an abuser himself!

It is amazing what you'll learn as time goes by and it will be free! Tuck it away in your file and at the right time in the negotiations discreetly let the opposition know you know -- then enjoy the look on his team's faces!

Let the private investigators on the big screen chase the un-faithful. Don't get sidetracked --

Beat Him At His Own Divorce!

18. DIVORCE EXPENSES

Divorces are expensive propositions! If people fully understood the cost in terms of financial, emotional and human resources, they would probably try to work things out and not jump into the divorce meat grinder as quickly as they do now. But the simple fact is that divorce is on the rise and this lesson is yet to be learned. So keep a good record of your financial losses.

From the moment you start responding to Mr. Wonderful's exodus, you will incur expenses. Telephone calls to relatives and friends, mail, copying, to say nothing of the legal and accounting fees that will start to mount up. Develop a system for recording them each month and do it religiously.

A simple ledger with five columns will suffice: item, amount, date, purpose and comments. For every expenditure enter this information. Appendix D contains a sample format if you would like to use it.

Sometimes divorce expenses can provide substantial leverage in your final settlement. Not only are the costs important, but sometimes the fact you had to make the expenditure sheds a negative light on your departed hubby. For example, if the kids need medical attention and you have to pay for it, that might speak to the issue of suitable parenting. Or, if there is a great deal of real estate that needs to be evaluated and the estimates are substantially different from the opposition's figures, the court might question his "fairness" as well as the actual determination of what your share is worth. By keeping a good record of the expenses you incur in financing his divorce, you may be able to enlighten the court about other issues peripheral to the actual expenditure as well as recover them in the settlement.

19. ARE YOU EVER REALLY DIVORCED?

With death there is finality -- at least in this world! A divorce may have many of the same emotional and financial strains as a death, but there is the additional burden of the lack of closure.

If Mr. Wonderful is divorcing you after a particularly lengthy marriage, complete with children, property and a lot of history, you will come to realize that it is never really final even though the ink has dried on the decree. You need to be prepared for this. It is almost like a sick joke after everything you went through in this divorce process that you never wanted in the first place.

Bumping Into Mr. Wonderful

You know what they say about a bad penny always showing up. Well Mr. Wonderful may not be worth that much, but you can bet he will keep showing up -- especially if you live in a small town.

There will be times when the children will have to interact with their father. If custody is an issue because you have younger children, you will undoubtedly have to interact with him yourself to some extent until the children are old enough to be on their own. The issues of what to do about holidays and vacations and family gatherings will continue to require attention as long as his shadow graces the earth!

If your children are adults, you still won't be off the hook! They might be able to deal with him themselves but what do you do when the grandkids come along, or there's a wedding or some other special event? You still have to deal with him. To make matters worse, he'll at some time want to include his newest "family member" in the festivities which means they have to address the fact he's sleeping with someone other than their mother! All this puts the kids in the middle. They have trouble adjusting to his new life and they don't want to alienate you as well.

If their father has some particular personality quirk such as always wanting to look good and maintaining his position as the "respected head of the family", your children will probably see right through him. That's healthy for them, but it also will mean they will come to lose respect for him which might manifest itself as some kind of physical ailment when they see him.

Most likely graduations, weddings, funerals, birthdays and holidays will become terrific opportunities to bump into Mr. Wonderful. He will probably want to play the parental role as if nothing has happened and since you are the other parent, you have the pleasure of dealing with that. If there are young grandchildren these events will become even more difficult because they don't know what to think. You and your children (their parents) may find yourselves trying to respond to children's questions one way and dealing with him another.

What if you are still in business with Mr. Wonderful? If you are, then you have probably already learned another lesson: "Family and business don't mix." In divorces with large amounts of property or a family business it may be difficult for one party to buy out the other. But since he wanted the divorce in the first place, let him start selling off properties to finance it. Or better yet, why don't you do as one woman did, start liquidating some of his favorite properties and give him a sense of urgency about matters!

Sometimes children realize that there is a substantial amount of money or property that they might inherit at some future date. You might see that your loving off-spring become a bit materialistic and don't want to alienate their father and run the risk of losing out on some of the future goodies. So their frequency of "bumping into" him may mysteriously increase and, to your aggravation, they may seem all too cheerful about it.

Memorabilia

One of the first things you will notice is that the treasured memorabilia of your lives together will become awkward trinkets. The jewelry that was given on anniversaries, birthdays and holidays will no longer have the rich patina of sentiment with which it was given -- or you thought it was!

So what do you do with the engagement and wedding rings? You could sell them to finance your portion of his divorce. You could give them back with a cryptic note at the moment his pen signs the divorce decree. There probably isn't much of a market for them among your children. How can they cherish or pass on something that no longer signifies the unity of their parents (unless they are highly materialistic as speculated before)? They don't make very good family heirlooms when there's no family tradition associated with them any longer.

Photographs of happier days like baby pictures, family portraits, birthday parties, holidays and the like can be real tear jerkers -- "Remember when we....?" So what do you do with them? One ex-wife went through the house and took down all of the pictures with him in them including the wedding pictures. She put them in a box and left them with his other things that he was picking up. She kept the pictures of herself and the kids and grandkids as well as any others that didn't have anything to do with him or his family. She cleaned out the albums, consolidated the pictures she kept and began a few new family traditions. After all, he left and she had the family!

If your Mr. Wonderful was a bit of a letter writer during your courting days and you kept them, be advised that they would make an outstanding fire starter on a cold night when you want a warm cozy fire in the family room. If you kept any of your replies, you might want to include them as well.

Memorabilia can be difficult to handle. You will need to be prepared to deal with it. But for all the trials artifacts from your past life can put you through, you also have the opportunity to begin some new traditions. Unlike Mr. Wonderful, you at least have a family to make those traditions with.

20. "WATCH OUT, SHE MIGHT BE CONTAGIOUS!!"

Have you noticed how good friends don't come around or call as often anymore? When you do go to parties isn't it strange how the women stay close to their husbands and how some of the husbands give you that certain look? Sometimes they're known as "listing husbands" (similar to leaky ships tipping to one side) -- kind of like Mr. Wonderful was now that you think back on it.

Some people will have come to regard you as a contagious person. The mutual friends you had before won't know what to say and if your hubby is a prominent person they won't want to upset him or appear to be taking sides. Wives will be nervous around you because they probably thought you had the "perfect" marriage and if it can happen to you, it might happen to them. The listing husbands might be seeing you in a new light and wondering why on earth your "Ex" left.

Don't be surprised if you are greeted with "Oh, how are *you?*" (Note the emphasis will be placed on the "you" when the speaker accentuates the word with a higher than normal tone of voice.) You can make a game out of this by counting the number of different ways people will say this same phrase. Some will come up real close and whisper in your ear with a tone of sincere familiarity.

Others will sound like a physician greeting a heart transplant patient for the first time after the operation. Many will try to be funny. Some will be truly interested either because they took your side during the divorce and never really could understand what you saw in him in the first place or perhaps they are looking for a bit of a change and you are the latest available person on the scene.

If you have the opportunity, try to be the mouse in the corner. You may be at a party or see some people in a restaurant. When they see you and you move on, try to hear what they say as you leave earshot. Their discussion may go something like this:

"She looks good. I wonder what she is doing now the divorce is complete."

"Didn't she have family in Alaska?"

"I heard she went on safari to Kenya with some rich shipper."

"I wonder what the children think of that!"

"I heard one became a Peace Corps worker in Bosnia and the other went to the North Pole in search of Santa's workshop!"

Some folks will treat you like you dropped off the end of the earth. They just can't believe you have a life without Mr. Wonderful. Maybe it's because they are afraid of what it would be like for them under such circumstances.

If you handle it right, you will learn two very important lessons. First, you'll find out who your real friends are and you can handle that accordingly. Second, you will see how superficial some people really are and who cares what they think anyway? One divorced woman was told more than once how hard this was on their friends! She rose to the high ground and said she understood since she had been in similar circumstances with other divorces herself.

In any case, have a giggle and count your blessings for not being like them!

21. SO WHERE DO YOU GO FROM HERE?

Well first you have to get through Mr. Wonderful's divorce. Hopefully some of the material in this book has been helpful -- it has for others. If you can take yourself out of the emotional side and treat the effort like a business project, that should help. But when that's done, what do you do?

Out of the Pan and Into the Fire

Many women did such a fine job picking out the first Mr. Wonderful that they repeat the process all over again and wind up back in the same fix. One woman was divorced for many years when she met a foreign gent whom she married after a substantial courtship. On her wedding day she expressed some doubts and a friend told her if she had doubts not to marry him. She did anyway and four years later divorced him and his overly controlling ways.

Another, suffered such low self-esteem following her divorce, she bedded everything in trousers for the next couple of years. Finally she realized she was getting nowhere and quit dating all together -- some swore she regained her virginity!

Don't jump out of the pan and into the fire. Don't repeat past mistakes. Think for yourself. Make a new life for yourself and learn to enjoy it and get comfortable with it.

A Few Facts About Your New Life

Whatever you do, understand a few facts of life following divorce:

#1 -- You do not have to do anything. Take your time and don't press the dating/mating ritual!

#2 -- Enjoy your family and if you do start dating, don't bring him around until you are sure your family is ready to meet him and he is ready to meet them.

#3 -- Your children may give you advice -- remind them who is still the mother!

#4 -- Your children will be ambivalent about your dating -- mothers don't do that kind of thing! -- but they want you to be happy too. So help them with the transition by easing them into it.

#5 -- Unfortunately, many (if not most) of the members of the male species that you encounter will have similar baggage as that your Mr. Wonderful carried -- especially if they are about the same age.

#6 -- You are now a new person following the divorce -- whether or not you want to be. Take advantage of it and don't repeat bad habits -- think for yourself, do what you want to do, stay away from control freaks, avoid overt flatterers, hold on to your money!

Remember the adage, "Today is the first day of the rest of your life?" Well it's true. You need to get on with your life and put the divorce behind you. There are changes to be made, new challenges, new joys, even new pains. So what's so different from any other life? Get out there and make a place for yourself because you

Beat Him At His Own Divorce!

EPILOGUE

There are very few certainties in life beyond death and taxes as Mr. Franklin observed over two centuries ago. However, in divorce there are some certainties that you can count on:

- No one ever wins -- everyone is hurt by divorce.

- You may not have wanted it, but you're stuck with it, so make the best of his divorce.

- If you can find a little humor in the tragedy it will help.

- Try to treat his divorce like a project to be completed soon.

- You can't do it by yourself -- get the right professionals but be sure they understand you are in charge.

- Find someone who can serve as your Project Manager, who is completely in your corner but will give you honest and direct feedback. Pay the person for his time.

- The short-term pain of fighting for what you deserve is less great than the long-term pain of wishing you had.

- You can use the management techniques in this book to help keep the whole mess from getting too out of control.

Now reread this book a couple more times. Muster all your resolve and courage. Swear you won't be upset again (at least not until the next time!) and,

Beat Him At His Own Divorce!

APPENDICES

APPENDIX A
SAMPLE MONTHLY EXPENSES FORM

Automobile Expense   _____
Babysitting   _____
Birthday Gifts   _____
Child Care   _____
Christmas Gifts   _____
Church Tithe   _____
Clothing   _____
Cleaning Supplies   _____
Credit Card Payments _____
Dental Bills   _____
Drugs   _____
Education Costs   _____
Electricity   _____
Eye Glasses   _____
Food   _____
Gas   _____
Gasoline   _____
Gifts   _____
Home Repairs   _____
Insurance
    Home   _____
    Life   _____
    Health   _____
    Disability   _____
    Other   _____
Lawn Care   _____
Loan Payments   _____

APPENDIX A (cont'd)

Medical Bills   _____
Mortgage   _____
Periodicals   _____
Pet Care   _____
Recreation   _____
Rent   _____
Savings   _____
Sundries   _____
Taxes
    Federal   _____
    State   _____
    Personal Property _____
Telephone   _____
Vacation   _____
Water Bill   _____
Other

_____   _____
_____   _____
_____   _____
_____   _____
_____   _____
_____   _____
_____   _____

APPENDIX B
SUMMARY PROPERTY INVENTORY FORM

Husband's Name: _____ SSI#: _____

Wife's Name: _____ SSI#: _____

Husband's Birthdate: _____ Wife's Birthdate: _____

Location of Safe Deposit Box: _____

Husband's Salary: $_____ Employer: _____

Wife's Salary: $_____ Employer: _____

Home Location: _____ Market Value: $_____

Checking Accounts

Number	Balance	Owner
_____	_____	_____
_____	_____	_____
_____	_____	_____
_____	_____	_____

Savings Accounts

_____	_____	_____
_____	_____	_____
_____	_____	_____

Stocks & Bonds

Item	Value	Owner
_____	_____	_____
_____	_____	_____
_____	_____	_____
_____	_____	_____

IRAs and Pensions:

_____	_____	_____
_____	_____	_____
_____	_____	_____

Life Insurance Policies

	Company/Policy No.	Face Amount	Cash Value
Husband's	_____	$_____	$_____
	_____	$_____	$_____
	_____	$_____	$_____
Wife's	_____	$_____	$_____
	_____	$_____	$_____

Vehicles

	Value	Owner
_____	$_____	
_____	$_____	
_____	$_____	

Tangible Personal Property

Item	Value	Owner
	$	
	$	
	$	
	$	
	$	
	$	

Real Estate

Property	Value	Owner
	$	
	$	
	$	

Gifts to Husband

Item	Value	Donor	Date
	$		
	$		
	$		
	$		
	$		
	$		

Gifts To Wife

Item	Value	Donor	Date
	$		
	$		
	$		
	$		
	$		
	$		

APPENDIX C

TASK PLAN FORMAT

Task	Product	Due Date	Assigned Person
_____	_____	_____	_____
_____	_____	_____	_____
_____	_____	_____	_____
_____	_____	_____	_____
_____	_____	_____	_____
_____	_____	_____	_____
_____	_____	_____	_____
_____	_____	_____	_____
_____	_____	_____	_____
_____	_____	_____	_____
_____	_____	_____	_____
_____	_____	_____	_____
_____	_____	_____	_____
_____	_____	_____	_____
_____	_____	_____	_____
_____	_____	_____	_____
_____	_____	_____	_____
_____	_____	_____	_____
_____	_____	_____	_____
_____	_____	_____	_____
_____	_____	_____	_____
_____	_____	_____	_____
_____	_____	_____	_____
_____	_____	_____	_____

APPENDIX D

SAMPLE DIVORCE EXPENSE FORM

Item	Date	Purpose	Amount	Comments

NOTES

NOTES

NOTES

NOTES

NOTES

NOTES